German Shepherd Dogs as Pets

A Complete Ultimate Guide

Facts & Information, where to buy, health, diet, lifespan, types, breeding, care and more!

By Lolly Brown

Copyrights and Trademarks

Disclaimer and Legal Notice

Foreword

Lauded as one of United States of America's most sought after dogs, the German Shepherd has captured many hearts with its notably high intelligence and its reliable capability. Developed and bred to be utilized and employed as a working dog, the German Shepherd, a relatively new canine breed, has reached a pinnacle of popularity.

Due to the unpopular association with the Germans during the first and second World Wars, the German Shepherd was once known and dubbed as the "Alsatian" in some parts of Europe and Great Britain.

The next chapters are geared toward important information and vital bits about the German Shepherd which can help you, decide if a German Shepherd is the canine you would want to add to your family mix.

You will also get to know about its characteristics and traits which will hopefully make you consider this breed as your pet.

Table of Contents

Chapter One: Introduction

The Deutscher Schäferhund, or the German Shepherd, is a working dog breed of medium to large size which originated from Germany. Time and again, the German Shepherd Dog has proven itself to be a loyal and trustworthy partner of human beings who once worked on the fields and once herded flocks of farm beasts. Although times have changed with the advent of technology and the industrialization of many countries, the German Shepherd continues to show its unmatched talents and innate skills to be crucial to jobs and tasks that would otherwise be difficult for humans to carry out on their own.

In the English language this fiercely loyal canine is officially recognized as the German Shepherd Dog and is oftentimes abbreviated as GSD. In Great Britain it was once known as the Alsatian. Its origins dates back to 1899; the German Shepherd Dog is a part of the Herding Group which is a collective working dogs group and was originally developed for sheep herding.

Owing to their collective intelligence, strength, obedience and trainability, German Shepherds have consistently been the preferred breed for a number of other countless tasks other than herding. They are used in jobs such as search-and-rescue, disability assistance, and detection of dangerous substances.

They play vital roles in police and military operations and continue to serve as bomb-sniffing dogs, supplies carriers, and even function as messengers on the battle field. It has proven itself to be a loyal and faithful companion to its human owners. These smart and easily trainable canines have staked their claim in show business and are often the popular choices to play characters in notable movie roles.

Unsurprisingly, the GSD is second on the list of the most-registered breed under the banner of the American Kennel Club. Meanwhile, at the Kennel Club in the United Kingdom, it is the fourth most registered breed.

Glossary of Dog Terms

AKC – American Kennel Club, the largest purebred dog registry in the United States

Almond Eye – Referring to an elongated eye shape rather than a rounded shape

Apple Head – A round-shaped skull

Balance – A show term referring to all of the parts of the dog, both moving and standing, which produce a harmonious image

Beard – Long, thick hair on the dog's underjaw

Best in Show – An award given to the only undefeated dog left standing at the end of judging

Bitch – A female dog

Bite – The position of the upper and lower teeth when the dog's jaws are closed; positions include level, undershot, scissors, or overshot

Blaze – A white stripe running down the center of the face between the eyes

Board – To house, feed, and care for a dog for a fee

Breed – A domestic race of dogs having a common gene pool and characterized appearance/function

Breed Standard – A published document describing the look, movement, and behavior of the perfect specimen of a particular breed

Buff – An off-white to gold coloring

Clip – A method of trimming the coat in some breeds

Coat – The hair covering of a dog; some breeds have two coats, and outer coat and undercoat; also known as a double coat. Examples of breeds with double coats include German Shepherd, Siberian Husky, Akita, etc.

Condition – The health of the dog as shown by its skin, coat, behavior, and general appearance

Crate – A container used to house and transport dogs; also called a cage or kennel

Crossbreed (Hybrid) – A dog having a sire and dam of two different breeds; cannot be registered with the AKC

Dam (bitch) – The female parent of a dog;

Dock – To shorten the tail of a dog by surgically removing the end part of the tail.

Double Coat – Having an outer weather-resistant coat and a soft, waterproof coat for warmth; see above.

Drop Ear – An ear in which the tip of the ear folds over and hangs down; not prick or erect

Entropion – A genetic disorder resulting in the upper or lower eyelid turning in

Fancier – A person who is especially interested in a particular breed or dog sport

Fawn – A red-yellow hue of brown

Feathering – A long fringe of hair on the ears, tail, legs, or body of a dog

Groom – To brush, trim, comb or otherwise make a dog's coat neat in appearance

Heel – To command a dog to stay close by its owner's side

Hip Dysplasia – A condition characterized by the abnormal formation of the hip joint

Inbreeding – The breeding of two closely related dogs of one breed

Kennel – A building or enclosure where dogs are kept

Litter – A group of puppies born at one time

Markings – A contrasting color or pattern on a dog's coat

Mask – Dark shading on the dog's foreface

Mate – To breed a dog and a bitch

Neuter – To castrate a male dog or spay a female dog

Pads – The tough, shock-absorbent skin on the bottom of a dog's foot

Parti-Color – A coloration of a dog's coat consisting of two or more definite, well-broken colors; one of the colors must be white

Pedigree – The written record of a dog's genealogy going back three generations or more

Pied – A coloration on a dog consisting of patches of white and another color

Prick Ear – Ear that is carried erect, usually pointed at the tip of the ear

Puppy – A dog under 12 months of age

Purebred – A dog whose sire and dam belong to the same breed and who are of unmixed descent

Saddle – Colored markings in the shape of a saddle over the back; colors may vary

Shedding – The natural process whereby old hair falls off the dog's body as it is replaced by new hair growth.

Sire – The male parent of a dog

Smooth Coat – Short hair that is close-lying

Spay – The surgery to remove a female dog's ovaries, rendering her incapable of breeding

Trim – To groom a dog's coat by plucking or clipping

Undercoat – The soft, short coat typically concealed by a longer outer coat

Wean – The process through which puppies transition from subsisting on their mother's milk to eating solid food

Whelping – The act of birthing a litter of puppies

Chapter Two: German Shepherds in Focus

This breed developed and christened by Von Stephanitz was to play a big role to the development of the GSD population as a whole. He called the canine, Deutscher Schäferhund, which when translated to English, literally means "German Shepherd Dog". This breed was named as such in keeping with the ideal purpose of helping shepherds in herding and securing sheep and other farm beasts.

During that time, all herding canines in Germany were referenced by this name; later, those dogs became known as Altdeutsche Schäferhunde or Old German Shepherd Dogs.

Interesting Facts about the German Shepherd

The handsomely smart GSD is a medium to large size dog and the breed standard height is 60-65cm at the withers for males and 55-60cm for bitches. They sport a domed forehead; its muzzle is long and square-cut with a black nose and very strong jaws. The GSD lively eyes are medium-sized and brown that carries an air of self-assuredness and intelligence. Its ears stand erect and are large, open and parallel at the front but are usually pulled back whilst in movement. The GSD has a long neck which is lowered when moving in a quick pace but is raised when excited and when on alert. The tail which reaches to the hock is bushy and thick.

The GSD has a two-layer coat and a thick undercoat that is dense and clings close. There are two accepted and recognized variants of the GSD coat which are medium and long. The gene which sports the long hair is recessive thereby making it rarer. The treatment of Long-haired GSD has stark differences and variations according to each association breed standards. Under the German and UK Kennel Clubs the dogs are recognized but are not allowed to compete with dogs sporting standard coated-dogs. This sort however is considered a fault amongst the American Kennel Club. The Federation Cynologique Internationale or FCI of Belgium has recently accepted the long-haired sort in 2010. The FCI lists the long-haired kind and has classified it as the B variety whilst the short-haired sort is classified as a variety.

Generally common amongst GSD colours are either red/black or tan/black. The variety of most colours have masks of black, black body markings which may range from an over-all "blanket" to the more classic "saddle". Variations of the rarer colors include pure black, pure white, liver, blue varieties and sable. The sable and all-black varieties are, according to most standards, acceptable. However, the liver and blue are seen as serious faults and the all-white is reason for instant disqualification from showing in conformation at all Specialty and Breed Shows.

Renowned for their impressive intelligence, German Shepherds were bred specifically because of this keen trait of theirs.

Author Stanley Coren wrote of them in the book he penned, The Intelligence of Dogs, and ranked the astoundingly clever GSD third for their innate intelligence, tailing Border Collies and Poodles, which top the list, very closely. He discovered that the GSD had the ability to pick up uncomplicated tasks after five repetitions. He also found out how the GSD is able to obey the first command given 95% of the time. Paired with their strength, this trait of obedience has made the breed of the German Shepherd desirable and make them successful candidates to work with respective law authorities as search and rescue dogs, guard dogs or police dogs. They are quick to learn and are able to carry out a variety of jobs and interpret instructions given to them better than breeds of other sort.

The watchful German Shepherd is a moderately active canine and is illustrated as self-assured in breed standards. Their sort is well-noted to display readiness to learn and a propensity for purpose. They are naturally curious about everything and everyone around them, making them excellent investigators. They are top-notch guard dogs and have assisted in many search missions.

If not socialized properly, a GSD can turn out to be too over-protective of its caregiver and family. A GSD will not be likely for a GS to be inclined to make new pals with your close friends much less, strangers. However, German

Shepherds are positively obedient, intelligent canines who are brave protectors of their caregivers.

Correct socialization can be managed if the GSD is trained early on in its life. Doing this will not only train your young German pup disciplines it will also help bring out and highlight its best qualities. Training a GS pup will also calibrate its protective characteristics and gear its skills toward both your advantages.

The German Shepherd Breed History

During the 1850s in Europe, efforts were executed to standardize dog breeds. Canines were bred to help preserve traits which helped these dogs to successfully carry out their tasks of protecting their flock of sheep wards from predators as well as to herd them from field to barn and vice versa. This was practiced amongst local communities in Germany where select dogs were bred by shepherds.

It was noted far and wide that the GS was a breed who possessed the necessary skills and abilities required herding sheep. It displayed intelligence, strength, speed and most importantly, a very keen sense of smell.

The outcome of this selection breeding was that the canines showed highly skilled aptitude to carry out these tasks well. It was noted that the canines differed from each other significantly in appearance and ability from one locality to the next.

Division and Disagreement

In 1891, Phylax Society was founded with intent to create development plans for native canine breeds in Germany. After three years and countless internal conflicts regarding what dog traits the society should promote, the society disbanded. These internal conflicts would pose a problem in the advancement of discussions about standardizing the breed.

The members were divided on what they believed should be promoted and bred in the canines. Some members believed that the canines should purposely be bred solely to work, whilst others pursued the notion that the canines should also be bred for its appearance.

While unsuccessful with their aim to standardize breeds, the Phylax Society paved the way and inspired dog aficionados after them to pursue the standardization of dog breeds independently. Tailing the rise of large, bustling, industrial cities in Germany a drop was noted in the predator population along with the occurrence of animal attacks.

This rendered sheepdogs to become redundantly unnecessary. Moreover, the cognizance of sheepdogs as an intelligent, versatile sort of canine commenced to increase.

The GSD Catches the Fancy of an Avid Aficionado

Ex-cavalry captain and former student of the Berlin Veterinary College, Max von Stephanitz, was a former member of the defunct Phylax Society, and he stood his ground believing that canines should be bred for employment. He extolled and explored the innate intelligence, ability and strength of the native sheepdogs of Germany but was unsuccessful in singling out a particular breed which satisfied his ideology of a perfect working dog.

Von Stephanitz attended a dog show in 1899 where he was presented to and met a canine given the moniker Hektor Linksrhein. A product of a few generations of selective breeding, Hektor absolutely fulfilled Von Stephanitz vision of what a working canine is to be.

He was very happy to witness the strength of the dog and was instantly taken with the intelligence of the handsome animal, its loyalty, beauty and stature that solidified Max's decision to purchase the canine Hektor instantly.

After taking ownership and committing to be guardian to the canine, Max changed the dog's name to Horand von Grafrath and Von Stephanitz proceeded to establish Verein fur Deutsche Schaferhunde or the Society for the German Shepherd Dog. The GS, Horand was the first canine added to the society's registry of breeds.

The Important Role of Horand to the Breed We Know Today

Horand went on to become the centerpoint of breeding programs and was paired with dogs owned by other society members who showed desirable traits and attributes. Horand was also bred with dogs from Franconia, Wurtemberg and Thuringia. The very important Horand fathered many pups, the most successful pup being Hektor von Schwaben.

Hektor von Schwaben was inbred with another of Horand's pups and this union produced Heinz von Starkenburg, Pilot and Beowulf. Pilot went on to later father eighty four puppies when he was inbred with other offsprings of Hektor. Inbreeding procedures were deemed fundamental in order to fix the traits they sought from the breed.

The original studbook of the German Shepherd, Zuchtbuch für Deutsche Schäferhunde (SZ), there are four Wolf Crosses. Found in two entry pages SZ No.41 to SZ No. 76. Beowulf's offspring were inbred as well and it is from these puppies that all German Shepherds of the present day draw genetic lineage.

It was through the uncompromising, strong leadership of Max von Stephanitz, it is held, that the society accomplished its goal of standardizing the breed. Von Stephanitz is credited therefore as being the creator of the German Shepherd Dog.

An Unpopular Name for a Popular Dog

The categorical translation of this name was adopted so it could be used in the official breed registry. However, at the end of the First World War it was observed that including the word "German" would harm the popularity of the breed owing largely to the anti-German sentiment of that era.

The United Kingdom Kennel Club officially renamed the breed to "Alsatian Wolf Dog", taking its name from the

French region of Alsace which bordered Germany. Hereafter, this name was later adopted by countless other kennel clubs around the world.

Sometime later, the "wolf dog" appendage was dropped from the title when breeders went on countless campaigns to remove part of the moniker which they believed may dissuade aficionados from acquiring and employing German Shepherds. These breeders were uneasy about this appendage added to its name and figured that the canine's legality and popularity would be greatly affected if they remain to be known as a wolf dog hybrid.

The moniker "Alsatian" stuck around for the next five decades until successful campaigns by dog enthusiasts in 1977 pressured the kennel clubs of Great Britain to allow the breed to once again be registered as German Shepherds. The name "Alsatian" would still appear in parentheses showing it as part of the formal breed and was hence removed altogether in 2010.

GSD's Use to Society

Lauded as one of the most intelligent and easily trainable canine's, the German Shepherd breed is a breed which is highly skilled and is possibly one of the most professional working dog breeds we will ever come across. The continued clamour for these canines has not let up and its popularity only has shown greater increase with time.

In this section you will discover the many jobs the German Shepherd is employed to do. You will discover its keen abilities that allow it to aid humans with their everyday needs. It will also reveal the unique traits of the GSD which makes it a favored breed amongst various sectors of society.

Senses and Sensibilities of the German Shepherd

The German Shepherd has been, and continues to be, a popular breed choice to employ as a working dog. They are specifically well-known for their contribution to police work and military operations to name a few of the jobs it courageously carries out. GSs are employed to track criminals, to patrol problematic areas as well as the detection and subduing of a suspect.

In addition to that, thousands upon thousands of German Shepherds have been flanking military personnel ever since they were found to be such effective scout partners. They are trained to patrol high-risk areas and are utilized to give warning to soldiers when enemies are present, booby traps, or other hazards which may post mortal danger to the troops.

These very intelligent canines have also been trained by different military forces to jump and parachute from an aircraft and act as anti-tank weapons. In WWII, they played a big role as messenger dogs, personal guard dogs and rescue dogs. A good lot of these dogs were taken in by foreign servicemen who became impressed by the GS intelligence and obedience.

This trustworthy canine is one amongst the most widely used breeds in a wide assortment of scent-work. These roles include cadaver search, narcotics detection, explosives detection, search and rescue, mine detection and accelerant detection dogs.

They are well suited for these roles of employment due to their ability to work without being distracted and their keen sense of smell. There was a period when the GS breed was exclusively chosen to be used by the visually impaired as seeing-eye dogs.

German Shepherds as Guide Dogs

In the 1920's, under the leadership of Dorothy Eustis, formal training for guide dogs began. The entire canine that is trained for this specific job was female German Shepherds. The results of a temperament testing showed that the

German Shepherds were superior in defensive behavior and aggression in contrast to Labrador Retrievers who scored higher on average in the ability to recover easily from frightening situations, cooperative behavior, emotional stability and friendliness.

These revealing results concluded that Labrador Retrievers were more suitable to work as a guide dog whilst German Shepherds were most suitable in police work and military operational tactics.

Presently, Golden Retrievers and Labradors are more frequently utilized to work as guide dogs; however there are still many German Shepherds which are being trained for the role of guide dog. 15% of the canines being trained by Guide Dogs of America are German Shepherd Dogs while the remainder of this lot is filled by Labrador Retrievers and Golden Retrievers.

In the great isles of the United Kingdom, The Guide Dogs for the Blind Association states that crosses between Labrador Retrievers and Golden Retrievers make the best guide dogs although they still train other breeds for this job along with German Shepherds.

In the United States, Guide Dogs for the Blind only train Golden Retrievers and Labrador Retrievers as well as crosses between these loyal breeds. In Australia, Guide Dogs Queensland exclusively trains Golden Retrievers and Labrador Retrievers for this role.

German Shepherds are still used in this present day to herd and tend sheep in fields and meadows next to crop fields or gardens. They are tasked to secure and patrol outskirts and boundaries to prevent sheep from damaging crops and trespassing. In Germany and many other places these skills are gauged in utility canine trials also called HGH herding trials for utility dogs.

The Mexican German Shepherd, Zuyaqui, regarded as the canine that was instrumental in the capture and seizure of the most drugs in the Mexican military and police history was put on display at the Sedena Narco Museum in Lomas de Sotelo, Mexico.

Chapter Three: German Shepherd Dog Requirements

Taking in a German Shepherd entails responsibilities which will fall on your shoulders. At this stage of your research you want to be able to determine if the personality and traits of the GS is suitable to you, your family and your existing lifestyle. This is but sound to determine at this point of your research. Every home has its own dynamics and dances to a beat of which is exclusively theirs, therefore, determining if the German Shepherd would make a suitable companion and house mate is imperative at this early stage of making a decision.

There are factors you will want to consider because just like other pets and humans, the German Shepherd has its own set of traits which are unique to their sort. To add to this; each animal has their own unique set of characteristics that may or may not be found in others. Your determination of what is and expectations of what is to come will be important things to determine.

Sundries and Equipment Your GSD Will Need

Your German Shepherd dog, once out in the world, will be biding time until it is able to join you and your family at home. It is imperative that you provide it with all the things it will require to feel welcomed and at ease to allow seamless transition into the family and the household.

You will need to make a considerable invest in food, a number of equipment, accessories, grooming tools, dog supplies, toys, and general sundries which will not only solidify the presence of the canine within the home, these will also be important purchases that will help integrate the GS canine to your family.

Here are some of the important things you need to shop for before you take home your new GS buddy:

Bed

The new addition to your family will need a place to rest its head just like you. Provide it with a sturdy bed, one in which it can comfortably lay in when it's all tuckered out and it's energy is running low. Give your GS dog a dedicated spot in the house to retreat to and recharge when much needed rest is required.

Dog Crate

A durable dog crate, if chosen properly, will serve both you and your furry buddy well for a very long time. Invest in a sturdy one as this will be a piece of equipment that will prove worthy of the money you spent over time. Transporting your GS canine to and from places will be a reality you will soon realize and you will definitely not want to put your canine buddy in danger riding in any sort of vehicle without any form of protection.

You will most likely want to bring your GS dog along for extended family trips or short term holidays so this will also conveniently double as its home away from home during trips and vacations.

Blanket

The word blanket can relay to a world of familiar comfort to anyone. And this too holds true for the German Shepherd. Give your GS dog a blanket it can snuggle into when days and nights become cold. This can be placed on the bed of the canine or be moved to a more social area of the home. It could also double as a bed for quick, energizing naps.

Stainless steel, slow-feeding bowls

In order to discourage your canine from wolfing down food and taking large gulps of water, utilize these convenient slow-feeding bowls for its meals and drink. The bowl is fashioned to promote slow-eating thereby allowing your canine the luxury of enjoying each morsel of food you set out for it.

A stainless steel feeding and drinking bowl will save you money in the long run and give you the peace of mind that the materials used to make the dishes are non-toxic and easy to clean.

Leash

You will need to make use of a leash on your GS dog while it undergoes training. This will also come in handy and useful when you take it out for much needed walks. Make sure to invest in one that is durable and that will last, especially for when your GSD comes into maturity. A full grown GSD will be powerfully strong therefore; a flimsy leash may find you chasing after your German Shepherd in the most inopportune of moments.

Fence

A collapsible fence can be utilized to create separation between existing pets and a new addition. It can be used to give the pet's sufficiently time to investigate and scout out each other; it serves as a safe barrier that will hinder them from getting any closer to each other before they are ready to share the same space. A fence can also be used to prevent the canine from wandering out of an open door or into an uncovered pool.

Toys

Your dog will be needing lots of toys to engage the curious and intelligent mind of your new GS dog buddy.

Using toys to stimulate the canine's mind is a strong recommendation and one you would wisely heed if you want to avert the dog's boredom from creating an awful mess of a wreck.

The clever GS is one who needs to be engaged one way or another - physically and mentally - or it will channel all that energy to inanimate things around that house which it can chew on, scratch at, dig on, and push around. Do not encourage this behavior, instead provide it with lots of toys it can play with which can be used as well during your own personal downtime with your new GS canine.

Grooming Brush

A good brushing of the GSDs coat is an essential routine you, or another caregiver in the family, will need to mind. The GSDs coat is thick and wiry; if not given the proper attention the coat will be prone to tangling and matting. The time when you give your GSD a good brush will also be a perfect opportunity to check its skin, belly and extremities.

Keep in mind that the overall health of any pet, whatever breed they may be, will be reflected in its coat and skin. A smooth coat, free of matting and tangles, is one indication of proper nutrition. A skin sans bald patches, rashes and nicks is a skin to be envied.

Make a habit of brushing your GSD coat to help promote the equal distribution of essential skin oils to stave off skin conditions or as a precaution, to detect the onset of any skin condition that may be harmful to your GSD.

Toothbrush

Your GS dog will need regular brushing to clean its teeth of plaque and food debris. Choose a toothbrush that will do the job right. Make sure that the brush fits comfortably in the GS dog's mouth and that it is strong enough to withstand any mischievous biting your GSD may give the brush. You will also need pet approved toothpaste to effectively clean the GS dog's teeth. Ask your vet about the sort of cleaning paste to use for cleaning.

Nail trimmer, or sander

Trimming your GSDs nail will come into the picture sooner rather than later. You might have to experiment on tools which your dog will respond to with the least resistance. Some dogs find it very uncomfortable when their guardians do the necessary work of trimming their nails, so it is important for you to observe and take mental notes as to which method of nail trimming it is agreeable to. When employing a cutter or guillotine, make certain that you cut above the pink of the animals nail.

Cutting through it can cause profuse bleeding and great discomfort to the canine. A sander can be gentler on a dog's senses, however, the continuous whirr of the machine may cause discomfort to the dog's keen hearing and it tends to heat up with prolonged use.

It is certain that you will find more things your German Shepherd will need to ensure a warm welcome and a happy union with you and your family. This would be a good time to network with experienced GS dog caregivers and guardians and find out what worked and didn't work for them.

Keep in mind that offered advice should be weighed and considered as no two dogs have the exact same needs. Ultimately only you and the immediate people it comes in contact with, on a daily basis, will be the ones who will know the GS canine best, therefore, more aware and mindful of its needs.

The Pros and Cons of Welcoming a GSD

The majestic German Shepherd Dog (GSD) is lauded for and is best known to be a courageously strong and an utterly obedient guide dog focused and dedicated to helping the disabled. They are also employed and valued as service dogs, flanking officers of the law, due to their innate tenacity, loyalty, intelligence and unwavering focus. They are often sought after to be protectors and guard dogs - a job they fill in well.

While they were primarily bred as a herding breed, GSDs can become outstanding, protective, family companions who will be willingly ready to display affection to its "wards". They possess a unique personality marked by a fearlessly direct expression. It carries itself with an air of visible self-confidence and a disinclination to make random, indiscriminate friendships.

They have a tendency to act indifferently when strangers are present and will most likely be aloof; however, once they pay you mind and decide to make friends with you, their devotion is for keeps.

The German Shepherd is a barker. This is due to their inherent protective nature, which is also the reason why they make such effective guard and police dogs. When a GSD connects and bonds with its new family it will display it protectiveness when approached by people - whether they be friends or strangers. This may be appropriate or inappropriate, depending on the situation presented, and the canine may not always be able to tell the difference or discriminate between these situations.

Here is where properly training the GSD, to recognize the presence of welcome and unwelcome individuals, comes into play. Proper socialization and early training will take care of the random, indiscriminate barking of the canine.

The GSD is a very smart breed who, with time and patience coupled with it being given the proper tuition, will easily be able to become well-integrated into regular social routines.

Aggressive tendencies and excessive shyness in GSDs are usually products of poor breeding, lackluster training, or possibly both. Once again, a stress on exploring the background and history of the canine, and committing to an appropriately suitable training protocol before making this leap of commitment is stressed and is something any potential GSD guardian should delve into deeper.

People without inclination, time or dedication to give full-time commitment to working with a German Shepherd should probably look elsewhere and select a breed more suited for their personality and lifestyle. Individuals who choose to willingly and openly devote energy, time to properly train their new GSD will find a tenfold return on their investment in the form of a loyal, well-adjusted family addition and lifelong companion.

Chapter Four: Acquiring Your Very Own German Shepherd

The future health and wellness of any pedigreed animal hinges on two things primarily; the history of its parents and the method employed by breeders during the mating period with nutrition and quality of food vying at a close second.

It is of utmost importance that, you, the future caregiver and guardian of this magnificent beast, research and determine the methods employed by breeders you will be doing business with. Stay away from pet stores and puppy mills. These sorts of operations propagate the instances of health issues seen in many animals. Discourage these places from furthering their shady operations, which is only set out to gain a quick buck, by not doing business with them.

To acquire a canine in the pink of health, never buy from an irresponsible breeder, a pet store or a puppy mill. The problems with irresponsible breeders run aplenty. If you choose to take this route you need to be aware that you could possibly be setting yourself up for a mountain of medical bills, avoidable worry and heartache. The sufferings of a GS pup who inherits medical conditions through unscrupulous breeding can be painful to live through and can certainly be avoided.

Irresponsible breeders pay no mind or care to how the breeding method is carried out. They do not take into account the possible future sufferings of the canine as a result of their improper breeding methods. They have no inclination to follow standard breeding procedures that will ensure the future good health of a GS pup. Unscrupulous breeders are out for one thing and that is to make a quick buck. Stay as far away from this sort and keep looking elsewhere.

Ask Lots of Relevant Questions - Rule Out Shady Breeders

To sift out the upstanding breeders from fly-by-night breeders, you will need to be observant and you will need to ask a lot of questions. Breeders who are only in it for the money will show no regard for the future well-being of the pup. They will not inquire about the family it will eventually be joining. It will not investigate if the home the pup is going to is a home that will welcome and care for it at any and all cost - they are only interested in you forking over the cash.

On the flip side, upstanding breeders will be concerned about the family and home the pup will be part of when it arrives. They will ask you some questions to determine if you are a sound and able guardian to this awesome creature. They would have inoculated and seen to the needs of the pup in the early days of its life before the GS pup is handed over to you.

These breeders of good repute will inquire of the GS imminent place in your family as well as the space you will have to provide for it. They will want to determine that the people who will be taking in the GS pup understand the challenges and rewards of sharing home with a GS. They will want to know that the young pup will be going to be part of a family who will extend it kindness, courtesy, respect, friendship and unconditional love. They will be curious to know if you have sought consult with a trusted and certified vet.

Seek out upstanding breeders who screen and test breeding canines and deem them fit and healthy to produce offspring. Make sure it is determined that the dogs are free of genetic diseases which may be passed down to future puppy litters. It is vital to know the history of the sire and bitch to make certain no congenital or hereditary disease plague the litter of pups. Check, as well, that the mating pair is of sound temperament and relatively relaxed.

Breeders of good standing and high repute will make no qualms in welcoming you to their facilities in order for you to be part of the whole breeding process. They will be open to answering questions you may have about the methods they employ during selection and mating. They will have kept records of milestones for when you are unavailable to be present. These breeders would be ready to offer useful information about the dam and sire as well as give you utilitarian tips and recommendations on how to effectively care for them.

When Adoption is An Option

Adoption is another avenue you may want to consider and should this be the route you choose to take, you will forever be doubly feel the rewards and benefits of taking in a GSD which you would have saved from a bleak future.

Be aware however that adopting a GSD, whether pup or full grown, will have its own set of challenges which may vary greatly from what one would expect when buying one from a breeder of good repute.

You will need to know that you will possibly be spending more money if the canine comes from a home which neglected to give it proper training, medical care, grooming attention and ample human interaction. You will also be set back financially if the canine has some sort of medical condition it has to live with. Should this be the case, it is advisable to ask as much as you can about the history of the GS you wish to adopt.

You will probably not get all the details of its history, which we discussed as important, as you would if buying from a reputable breeder but your open heart and willingness to take on the care of an ill pet (as well as a deep well of resources) will be just what a rescue pet needs.

On the bright side, once in the fold of your welcoming family, your GS rescue dog would have been given a new lease in life and a stay from a bleak and an uncertain future. Given your pure intentions and ready willingness to take in a rescue GS, integration may not be as tough as it would seem. You would have done a major good deed which puts you in the solid. This is just another of the great rewards and tiny perks of being guardian to a German Shepherd dog - and a GS rescue dog, at that, too.

Once your new, intelligent German Shepherd rescue understands what you have done for it, it will not think twice about expressing and showing its undying gratitude through its fierce loyalty and loving companionship for a very long time.

List of Breeders and Adoption Sites:

American Kennel Club
<http://marketplace.akc.org/puppies/german-shepherd-dog>

World Class GSD
<http://www.worldclassgsd.com/>

Puppy Spot
<https://www.puppyspot.com/breed/german-shepherd/>

Pet4Homes
<https://www.pets4homes.co.uk/sale/dogs/german-shepherd/>

Lancaster Puppies
<https://www.lancasterpuppies.com/puppy-search/breed/german%20shepherd>

Adoption

Southern California German Shepherd Rescue
<http://socalrescue.org/>

Adopt a Pet

<http://www.adoptapet.com/s/adopt-a-german-shepherd>

GSD Rescue

<http://www.gsdrescue.org/>

Pet Finder

<https://www.petfinder.com/dog-breeds/german-shepherd-dog>

Southeast German Shepherd Rescue

<http://www.southeastgermanshepherdrescue.com/>

Carolina German Shepherd Rescue

<http://www.southeastgermanshepherdrescue.com/>

Second Chance - German Shepherd Rescue

<http://www.scgsr.org/>

Networking - A Necessity

You may start networking with experienced GS guardians, expert dog handlers, dog trainers, your local vet and while at it, check out breeders online and read feedback from previous clients. You could also do a real solid and rescue a GS from a shelter. This avenue is possibly the most heartwarming manner to have a loyal GS join ranks in your family. A rescue dog will not be shy in expressing its gratitude through its friendship and loyalty to you and your kinfolk.

Chapter Five: Caring Guidelines for German Shepherds

The wellbeing and health of the German Shepherd hinges on a number of important factors and for which you will be mostly responsible. Remember that taking in a new life to care for comes with its rewards and its challenges. You need to be mentally, physically and financially ready to raise your new addition successfully.

Nutrition is the biggest factor of the lot. Feeding your GSD nutritionally sound food will not only ensure its healthy growth, it will also give the canine the security it needs as it comes to understand you to be the provider of the household - the Master of the Domain, so to speak.

A Daily Workout

German Shepherds are built for swift action and graceful maneuvers having been originally bred to herd flocks day in and out. In today's modern setting this equates to lots of much needed exercise to burn off all that pent up energy.

If left alone for too long sans physical activity and exercise, brace yourself for trouble in what should instead be paradise. Remember that you will be taking in a feisty, active canine whose intelligence demands for it to be occupied and engaged when not asleep or at rest. To avert boredom and the destruction of your favourite lounge chair, Wednesday pumps, or your Oxford browns, make it a point to regularly engage your faithful GS in play. This not only benefits both of you with some much needed exercise, it also affords you some quality bonding time to catch up with each other.

German Shepherds, due to their propensity to lead, are barkers like many other herding canines. Barking in itself doesn't necessarily pose a problem until it becomes the result of boredom and causes disruption. Here is where training comes in to save the day. The dog obedience training should include the provision for the dog to respond to the "QUIET" command when told, in fact, this should be right up there as one of the first important commands with which it should be familiar and heed.

The German Shepherd and You - Shared Activities

If you are away from home regularly or for extended periods of time, then you will want to rethink acquiring a GS. This is a good time to recall that the GS can be quite touchy about being left alone. It can easily become bored or anxious when left on its own and will likely express their dismay and disapproval in manners you won't find amusing - like chewing on furniture or shoes, or digging up planters and/or flower beds and loud, continuous barking that may set off your neighbors.

It is imperative to keep the GS busy by giving it responsibilities. Whether working, playing or learning, be reminded that the GS will require physical exercise and intellectual stimulation to stay efficient. It does not sit still for very long and will begin to look for things to keep itself entertained and amused. Being a smart and active dog it will be important for any would-be caregiver to know that the feisty GS will need stimulation of the body and mind to help it thrive and maintain its positive traits.

A daily traipse outside for a brisk run, a quick game of catch or Frisbee will all do the trick of helping your GS stay relaxed. Make sure that you seek out a reputable and successful trainer to work with you and your young GS because mental stimulation through sessions of training will be a necessary requirement for its discipline and overall well-being.

Promoting Positive Socialization - Start Training Young

In order to raise a well-behaved dog and promote positive socialization skills, a would-be guardian needs to introduce the canine to a variety of situations in order to expose it early to different scenarios and help it gain familiarity and footing of its expanding surroundings as it grows.

Introduction to canine training at the early stages of puppyhood is one sure fire way of preparing a GSD for its introduction into your world and the rest of society. Not only will you give your GS puppy an edge as you ready it for its debut to spaces beyond your home and backyard, you will also be instilling the trait of discipline to it which will but enhance and enrich its innate talents and abilities. The early stages of training teach your young GS pup social manners and hone its skills which may seem absent or dormant at this stage of its life.

It has been noted in many studies that teaching any skill at a young age gives the learner the advantage of higher intelligence and is observed to fare better during social interactions.

German Shepherds are notorious for being wary of strangers and will be aloof when in the presence of strange people. Being in new surroundings can also cause some GS to display foreboding anxiety and/or excessive excitement. Avert bad traits from flourishing in the canine, being passed down and occurring in future GS litters (select a reputable breeder). Curb these behavioral issues and channel these traits of misgivings in a positive way by taking him out to places where he can roam freely under your trained and watchful eye.

Give it a chance to explore a strange place and be patient with it as it learns its way around places and people. Begin obedience training for your would-be GS early and start him off when he is a pup. It will not only teach him the niceties of canine manners it will also allow him to get used to being in different locations whilst in the company of different canines and people.

To Leash or Not to Leash? - When to Keep the Leash Off

Yes, the German Shepherd is an excellent watchdog but never make the mistake of tethering or leashing your GS canine to a post or pole. This method of restraint will almost definitely lead to your frustration and your GS aggression.

Limit outdoor forays to a minimum with you supervising the trip outdoors. Do not make the mistake of leaving your GS to roam free on its own in the neighborhood to avoid complaints and to avoid warring with other canines in the area.

Your new GS buddy will be most happy living indoors with the rest of the family members. Be sure you allow it access to a large, fenced in yard to romp and run around in so that it can spend some of its innate energy. Keeping your GS canine indoors will require you to make space for it inside the house.

Be sure to give it delegated spaces around the house for it to retreat to when all tuckered out from a day of romping. Place its crate in a relatively tucked away but social area of the home like a hallway or under an indoor planter. Make provisions for its sleeping area where it can lay its large, intelligent head down at the end of the day.

Make space in the family kitchen and provide your GS an area where it can eat its meals in peace. Be sure to choose slow-feeding bowls to your GS to discourage it from wolfing down its food too quickly. Get the stainless steel sort of feeding bowl as this will less likely deteriorate with extended use.

Biting and Aggression

If a German Shepherd is well trained and properly socialized then expect it to pose no harm to you or anyone else. Each year an estimated 4.5 million people living in the USA is said to get bitten by dogs, this according to the Centre for Disease Control (CDC). German Shepherds, Chow chows, and other bully breeds are blamed far less often than any other breed.

A 1999 Australian report provides statistics reflecting German Shepherds to be the third most likely breed to attack a person in some Australian locales. Although weighing their popularity in factor, the percentage of the GSD attacks takes a dive at 38th lagging behind Bloodhounds and Pit Bull Terriers.

Dangerous Encounters, a National Geographic Channel television show, reported that the bite of a German Shepherd has a force of over 1060 newton. That's a lot of bite compared to that of a Labrador retriever, a Rottweiler and a human.

Coat Care and Grooming

Originally bred to assist farm hands and to herd flocks in regions that experience and go through seasons of harsh, cold climates, the German Shepherd's medium-length, double coat gets the job done right of keeping the canine warm and dry. Its coat helps insulate the canine from extreme cold temperatures and unpredictable sudden downpours. Resistant to picking up dirt and burr, its coat also protects the canine during the winter months when its fur serves the purpose of keeping it comfortably snug from the conditions mother nature doles out when it reaches out with frosty fingers.

Shedding

The GS has earned the nickname "German shedder" for good reason - these loyal dogs are famous shedders and will need attentive brushing and grooming to maintain a silky, soft coat and promote proper distribution of essential skin oils to its dermis. You will need to invest on a brush and pick up a reliable vacuum from the store. Don't scrimp on these sundries as you and your GS will be using them for a long time to come.

Put some money on a strong, sturdy crate which your canine will be using for a long time. Not only is it an ingenious manner of house training your GS puppy, it also aids to train him to stay calm and contented when separated from his guardians. This is highly recommended for the GS who can experience extreme anxiety when left alone, and who tends to go through separation anxiety when parted from its caregivers.

Chapter Six: Nutritional Needs of German Shepherd Dogs

Just like humans, dogs are unique individuals with specific quirks and needs that vary and differ from one canine to the next. As with food, they will not all require the same amount of food. How much your mature GS eats will largely hinge on its age, size, metabolism, built and activity level. A highly active dog will definitely need more nourishment than a stoic couch potato canine.

The quality of dog food you purchase and feed it also plays a factor in the amount of food you should set out for it. The higher quality sort of dog food will most certainly go toward nourishing your canine and as a result you won't need to put out as much of it into your dog's feeding bowl.

Proper Food and Nourishment Equates to Overall Wellbeing

You read earlier in this book that the assurance of a GSD leading a healthy and long life hangs on two primary factors; one is the accuracy and soundness of the clinical history of the German Shepherd's sire and dam, and the other, equally important factor, is the quality of food it is fed.

Choosing the right foods to feed your GSD will be an important decision you will make each time you go out and shop for its food. You will have to make choices and commit to providing the nourishment it would need to allow it to thrive and attain its fullest capacity in terms of its natural talents and abilities.

Making sound choices on food selection you serve to it will visibly reflect on the appearance, physique, temperament and abilities of your new GSD. Be sure to educate yourself about foods that are good for your GS pup or canine. Stay away from all the marketing hype meant to disguise unnecessary ingredients behind flowery label-wording and photos portraying lofty imaginings of seemingly happy, smiling pets.

Make the effort and be the frontline in giving your GS dog the nourishment it needs and requires. Find out about food manufacturers and their methods of producing pet food and what ingredients are put in the mix. Be aware of ingredients which may be of no use or be harmful to your GS dog.

Consumers of today have an unlimited number and quite a variety of food choices when it comes to providing food for the GSD. Gone are the days of bland and tasteless, genetic puppy food. Long has it been since adult dogs were fed one-flavor-meals.

Pet supply stores, internet retailers and grocery aisles teem with products that carry and promote various pet food brands from which to choose.

A GSD thrives and lives a happy life when on a well-balanced nutritional diet. When provided with an excellent array of nutritious food the GSD's skin is supple and soft, the coat grows full and thick, its ribs are not visible to eyes (not skinny) and are covered by skin that is taught and tight. His energy is apparent, infectious as it is boundless.

Commercial Food

Research led by commercial pet food manufacturers has resulted in heightened public awareness and knowledge of a canine nutritional requirement. These studies have also taught pet guardians on how food helps a dog live fully rather than merely existing. The sad truth is that not all commercially available dog foods are of high quality.

Up on the high end of the spectrum are foods produced with nutritious, human-grade ingredients which are engineered and produced to meet a canine's specific needs. On the other hand, ranking very low on the chart are low end food products which are concocted with poor sources of protein, a whole lot of useless fillers that may lead to obesity or malnutrition, as almost indigestible vitamins and minerals that do not the canine any good.

Learn To Decipher Labels

It can be challenging to understand any label we, as consumers, read. It is almost as if manufacturers don't want us to understand what is in the food we are putting on dishes and bowls! However, if you are canny enough and do your research, you will be able to identify several key point to zero in to as you try to figure out what is in the can, bag or package.

Learn to read the nutritional chart on each package and recognize key words that would indicate the quantity and quality of the ingredients used. You should also learn to recognize the type of dog and the specific life stage for which the food was produced.

There are some pet food producers who may switch up the ingredients and the ratio of ingredients with each batch, depending on what is available. These foods are tagged and labeled as a "variable formula diet".

A food which varies from one batch to the next also suffers in nutritional quality and this can result to the ill-health of the canine. A fixed formula, or a recipe which is constant, is able to provide the quality of food a canine needs but can be quite costly.

Quality manufacturers of high-grade, premium canine food put in a lot of money investing in the research and development of specific nutritional requirements for select subsections of the canine sphere. The supplements and ingredients involved in the producers' designer formulations are proprietary secrets which they do not care to disclose to the end consumer or to other pet food manufacturers for that matter. They are, however, based on available research as well as feeding trials.

Wet, Semi-Moist or Dry Foods

On top of learning to read labels, understanding the ingredients, buying food nutritionally sound for your GS's consumption, you will also need to make choices of whether to feed your canine wet, semi-moist and dry dog food.

Dog foods which come in cans are easy to store, very tasty and contain very little, if any, preservatives. Because of this, canned foods are to be consumed within 30 minutes of serving or it runs the risk of turning rancid. Canned foods are the most expensive commercial food choice. Being soft, the food does not aid in keeping the canine's teeth clean.

Semi-moist foods are stored in bags and are chewier in consistency. They have a shorter shelf life as compared to dry foods. These foods also contain more sugar to help maintain the soft consistency of the morsels. These foods also often contain food coloring to mimic the appearance of human food. Some canine's experience difficulty metabolizing these foods and the outcome, no pun intended, is softer stool and/or frequent soft bowel movement.

The least expensive of your choices is the commercially produced dry food. This sort promotes healthier gums and teeth and enjoys a longer shelf life compared to wet or semi-moist food. One common complaint, of the past in relation to dry foods, was that dogs did not fancy them because of its bland taste. Many dogs, unless fed this sort of food early in its life, would not be eager to have meals. However, stiff competition on palatability amongst pet food manufacturers had made this a thing of the past.

Homemade Meals vs. Natural Feeding

As more and more pet guardians demand the best of high grade ingredients for the sustenance of their dogs, many manufacturers stepped up to the plate and come out with impressively comprehensive lines of natural pet foods. In relation to this, countless pet guardians have opted to feed their dogs food made at home which may consist of a combination of cooked and raw ingredients, or an all-raw diet.

There are guidelines to be followed in order for an all-natural dog food to be labeled all-natural. These guidelines state that all ingredients as well as components of the ingredients present in the food must be naturally made. If any of the components are synthesized chemically, this must be stated clearly on the label.

Homemade meals are prepared diets commonly recommended by holistic veterinarians and would include cooked or raw meats, whole grains, raw vegetables and an assortment of nutritional supplements. A recipe from a vet, who has expertise in nutrition, if followed in accordance, can be an extremely healthy choice for your GS.

There are a number of drawbacks to consider should you be thinking about feeding your GS a purely homemade diet. As with preparing for your own meals, making homemade meals for your canine will take a considerable chunk of your time.

You can try to simultaneously prepare food for the family and for the canine, but be sure you do not get confused with what goes into which pot. Your canine's meals will need pre-planning just like your weekly family meals. If you are not prepared to sacrifice a good deal of your time cooking up a storm in the kitchen, you may want to seek the help of another family member who is equally committed to the care of the GS. Otherwise, you may want to consider an alternative route to feeding.

The required ingredients of a homemade meal must be purchased fresh, therefore costly. Most important of all, homemade diets must be made with utmost consistency, never veering away from the said recipe with substitutions. Variances in quantity is strongly discouraged if not outright unacceptable as such measuring and weighing ingredients are to be carried out with utmost care.

Whether you choose one method or the other, you will need to consult and work with your veterinarian regarding what you feed your GS pup. More so if you decide to make homemade meals, because your vet will not only be able to provide you with a recipe, they will also be able to tell you where to find sources of minerals, vitamins and ingredients you need to add to the homemade meal mix to provide your GS dog well-balanced meals.

Keep in mind that you will need to follow the vet's recipe, not doing so will do your GS more harm than good. Remember to keep measurements exact and that there are to be no substitutions specially if not approved by your vet.

Supplementing the Diet of Your GS

Theoretically, there is no requirement for additional supplements to your dog's' diet if a food is labeled complete and balanced - unless, of course, prescribed by your vet.

When feeding your GS you will be required to add a number of supplements to your GS daily diets in exact and precise measurements.

The determination of whether or not your GS needs additional supplements should be made with the assistance of your vet. You should never try to supplement the diet of your GS without consulting your vet as they will be best suited to consider the pros and cons of the effects of a specific supplement and determine what amounts the canine needs.

Feeding Pups and Adolescents

The GS breed is considered to be a large breed and perhaps because of its rapid growth, it has been hounded by abnormalities throughout its existence. Many breeders take great care and maintain accuracy and consistency on how and when they feed their pups and young dogs - mindful to not overfeed and instill obesity, which would put greater strain on the dogs' joints. They are also concerned about food extremely rich in nutrients that they promote alarmingly rapid growth. GS dogs that grow too fast are more likely to suffer from an array of bone and joint conditions.

There are a number of recommended methods to successfully feed your GS as tried out by some breeders. There are breeders who recommend feeding the canine premium puppy food until the dog is six months old, at which time they recommend switching to a premium quality dog food for active adults. You should give the puppy meals which are nutrient rich in the early stages of the canine's development and later, a leaner food sort which will stave off unwanted overgrowth.

Feeding a puppy premium large-breed puppy formula up to one year of its life then switching to a premium large-breed adult formula, is another method of giving your GS nourishment.

Figuring out the amount of food to feed your GS pup is another thing you will have to determine. One popular way to find out is using the 30-minute method. It is an easy as it is popular. To find out how much to feed your GS pup, measure out 3 cups of dry canine food and put this in the puppy's bowl. Give your pup access to the bowl of food and have it eat as much as it can within a thirty minute period.

Measure how much food was left in the bowl after the 30 minute period. Deduct this from the original 3 cups you measured out initially and you should have the appropriate amount of food that your puppy will need. Do this for about 2-3 days to get a more accurate measurement.

One of the leading causes of aggression in puppies is hunger, so it is equally critical for you to feed your GS enough food. The most common behavioral problems guardians complain of and vets hear about usually stems from inappropriate feeding - be it too much or too little.

Water - Fresh and in Abundance

Water is necessary to your German shepherd's system, to aid in digestion, to flush the toxins out, and to help maintain a constant body temperature. In order to consistently maintain the freshness of food and water your GS eats and drinks, always remember to keep all feeding and water bowls clean and dirt free.

Puppies as well as dogs can lose a considerable amount of water through exercise, panting and a rise of temperature when outdoors. If a dog is dehydrated by more than 12% it will die.

Having access to fresh, cool water allows your GS to maintain the correct water balance on its own by allowing it to drink when it needs to replenish liquid in its system. The absence of fresh water available at any given time of the day may lead to your GS to develop a bad habit of gorging on water, gulping huge quantities of it.

Keep in mind that, when considering the long term health and overall well-being of your GS, the quality of food you feed your dog will make all the difference. Feeding it premium, quality food will allow them to thrive better, their coats will be healthy, rich and plush, and they will incur fewer bouts with allergies, have fewer medical problems and will develop a healthier disposition and a happier personality.

Schedule, Frequency and Amounts

It is recommended that you set out 2 scheduled meals for your GS canine. 3 to 4 cups of high-quality, grade a dry food canine can be divided in two portions which you can serve your faithful buddy during meals should suffice.

Observe your dog and if it begins to show signs of weight gain, cut back on the portions you give. If he is looking scant, take note and make a mental note to put in a little more into his bowl.

To determine if your GS canine has tipped the scales and is overweight, use the hands-on test. Rest the palm of your hands on its body, placing your thumbs along its spine as your fingers fall slightly to the side and thumbs along its spine gently slide your palms along and down the sides of its body. You must be able to feel its ribs under a layer of muscle. If you can visibly see its ribs your dog is too thin. If undetectable under rolls of fat, then you will have to help it regain its healthy built and put it on a diet.

Remember that you will each be somewhat dependent on each other on a certain level. Be there for your canine buddy as it would be for you.

You will be required to pay particular attention and give thoughtful care with the feeding and exercising your new GS pup as they grow rapidly and gain considerable weight between the ages of four to seven months. This period of growth spurt makes them prone and vulnerable to bone disorders. Your furry, new GS pup addition will thrive well on a high-quality, low-cal diet (that is about 22 to 24 percent protein and 12 to 15 percent fat that will assist in preventing it from growing too fast.

Joint problems will surely be an avoidable, painful medical condition that the young GS pup will be susceptible to if it is overfed. Over-feeding your GS will result in him packing on unhealthy, unnecessary pounds that if left alone can only lead to health issues you would not want your canine to endure. Keep him active and alert by initiating and encouraging playtime.

Limit the ration of in between meals to a minimum - if you feel compelled to reward your GS with treats, factor in the nutritional values of the snacks you give it and subtract that nutritional value amount from the values of the scheduled meals you will be serving your GS. Keeping him on a feeding schedule will be one of the many responsibilities a caregiver will have to observe. Early training will allow the canine to learn to understand rules and allow it to develop and exercise self-discipline.

Chapter Seven: Showing Your German Shepherd

In order to show your German Shepherd dog you have to make sure that he meets the requirements for the breed standard and you need to learn the basics about showing dogs.

In this chapter you will receive information about the breed standard for German Shepherd breeds and you will find general information about preparing your dog for show.

General Appearance

An initial presentment of a good German Shepherd is that of an agile, well-muscled beast, alert, strong and full of life and vigor. It is well built and balanced, harmonious in development of the forequarter and hindquarter. Rather than tall, the dog sports a long physique, presents an outline of curves that are smooth rather than showing angular and is deep-bodied.

It is not spindly but looks rather substantial giving off the impression, whether in motion or at rest, of possessing nimbleness and muscular fitness minus any appearance of soft living or clumsiness. The ideal canine is stamped with an appearance of nobility and quality - hard to define, but undoubtedly true when present. Secondary sex traits are strongly recognized and each animal emits a definite impression of either femininity or masculinity, according to its gender.

Temperament

This breed possesses a unique personality marked by fearless and direct, however, not hostile, expression. The canine should be approachable, silently standing its ground and displaying willingness and confidence to meet overtures without making them itself. It is well poised, but when the situation calls for it, alert and eager; both willing and fit to serve in a capacity as watchdog, companion, herding dog, blind leader, or guardian, whatever circumstances demand its role to undertake. The dog is not to be timid, shrinking behind its handler or caregiver; nor should it display nervousness, looking upward or about with an anxious expression or displaying nervous ticks or reactions, like tucking its tail between its hindquarters, to strange people, sounds and sights. Atypical of good character is displaying a lack of confidence under any variation of surrounding.

These deficiencies mentioned above when displayed, which gives off the traits of shyness has to be penalized as very severe faults and any dog showing pronounced indications of these traits has to be excused from the show ring. It has to be made possible for the judge to see and observe the canine's teeth and to determine that both its testicles are in fact, descended.

A German Shepherd dog that makes an attempt to snap at or bite the judge has to be disqualified. The ideal working dog is an animal with a character which is incorruptible paired with physique and gait fit for the arduous work that makes up its primary purpose.

Substance, Proportion and Height

The desirable height for males at the tip of the utmost point of the shoulder blade is 24 to 26 inches; as for the bitches, 22 to 24 inches. The handsome GSD is longer in physique than it is tall, with the most desirable proportion as 10 to 8 1/2. The length is scaled from the tip of the breast bone or prosternum to the back edge of its pelvis, the ischial tuberosity.

The suitable long proportion is not derived from its long back but rather, from the overall length in relation to its height, which is attained by measuring the length of the forequarter and the length of the hindquarter and withers, when viewed at profile or from the side.

Head

The head is to be cleanly chiseled and must stand noble and strong sands coarseness, but above all is it not fine but must be in proportion with the body. The male head is notably distinct and masculine. That of the bitch is to be distinctly feminine.

Its expression is intelligent, composed and keen. Almond shaped eyes are medium in size, are not protruding and set slightly obliquely. The colour is as dark as it can get.

Ears are in proportion to its skull and are moderately pointed. The ears are open toward the front and are displayed erect when at attention. Viewed from the in front, the most ideal carriage is one in which the centre lines of the ears, are at parallel with each other and are perpendicular to the ground.

A canine with hanging ears or those which are cropped has to be disqualified. When viewed from the front, the forehead is to only be moderately arched and the skull is to slope into the long and wedge-shaped muzzle without abrupt stops.

The muzzle is strong and long, with its top line parallel to the utmost topline of its skull. The nose leather is to be black. A canine with a nose which is not predominantly black has to be disqualified. The lips are to be firmly fitted with jaws which are strongly developed. Its teeth are 42 when counted - 20 upper and 22 lower - and are developed strongly. The teeth meet in a bit that scissors and is part of where the inner surface of the upper incisors engage and meet part of the outer surface of the lower incisors.

A level bite or an overshot jaw is undesirable. A jaw displayed as undershot is a disqualifying fault. Complete dentition finds favorable results and judgment. Any missing teeth apart from primary molars are considered a serious fault.

Neck, Topline and Body

The GS neck is to be muscular and strong, relatively long and clean-cut, in good size proportion to the head and sports no signs of loosely folded or hanging skin. When the canine is excited or at attention, its neck is carried high and its head is raised; otherwise its typical carriage of the head is forward as opposed to up but it shows a little higher than the utmost top of the shoulders, especially in motion.

The GS withers are high and slopes into its straight back. The back should show straight, and should be strongly developed sans roach or sag and must be relatively short. The structure of the whole body is to give of an impression of solidity sans bulkiness and an impression of depth.

Beginning at the prosternum, the chest is to be carried well and must be well-filled well down between the legs of the GS. The chest is never shallow, but must be capacious and deep, with substantially enough room for the heart and lungs. The chest is carried forward smartly with the prosternum displaying ahead of the shoulder when viewed from the side.

Abdomen and Ribs

Ribs are sported long and well sprung. Ribs are neither too flat nor barrel-shaped and should be carried down to the sternum that should reach the canine's elbows. Proper ribbing permits the elbows to move back freely when the canine is at a trotting pace. Ribs that are developed too round will cause interference and will throw the elbows of the canine out; ribs too flat or too short causes elbows to be pinched. Ribbing is to be sported well back so that the canine's loin is relatively short.

The GSDs abdomen is not paunchy but is firmly and staunchly held with the bottom line showing to be moderately tucked up in the loin. When viewed from the top, the loin is to be strong and broad. When viewed from the side an undue length between the final rib and the thigh, is undesirable. It is to display as gradually sloping and croup long.

Tail

Its tail is to be bushy, with the rearmost vertebrae extending at least up to the hock joint. It is to be set smoothly into the croup of the canine and is to show rather low than high. When at rest, its tail is to hang in a moderately slight curve much like a saber. Occasionally carried to one side, a slight hook is faulty only if it interrupts and mars the overall look and appearance of the GS.

When in motion or excited the curve of the tail is accentuated and the tail is raised, however it must never curl forward beyond a vertical line. It the tails shows clumpy ends resulting from alkalosis, or is too short, are serious faults. A GS canine sporting a docked tail is to be immediately disqualified.

Forequarters

Obliquely angled and proportionately long is to be the appearance of the GSDs shoulder blades; the placement of the shoulders are to be positioned forward and not laid in flat. The upper arms of the GS are to join the shoulder blade at an approximate right angle. Both its upper arms and shoulder blades are strongly muscled.

The forelegs of the GS, when viewed from all sides and angles should show to be straight and the bone as oval rather than round. The pasterns are springy, strong and angulated from the vertical at approximately a 25-degree angle. Claws on the forelegs may be eliminated but are normally left alone. The feet are to be compact and short, with well displayed arched toes that are on firm pads which are thick; its nails are dark and short.

Hindquarters

The overall assembly of the thigh when viewed from a profile (or from the sides) is to be broad with either upper and lower thigh muscled well, forming as close as possible at a right angle. Parallel to the shoulder blade is the upper thigh bone while the lower thigh bone matches parallel to the upper arm.

The unit between the foot and the hock joint - or the metatarsus - is to show strong, short and tightly articulated. If any, the dewclaws would be eliminated from the hind legs of the canine.

Coat

Ideally, the GSD sports a medium length, double coat of fur. As dense as it can possibly get, the outer coat is to sport straight hair, harsh to the feel and lying close to the body of the GS. Permissible is an often wiry texture and a slightly wavy outer coat.

The neck of the GS is to sport comparatively longer and thicker hair from the rest of its body. The whole head, inclusive of the GS foreface and inner ear, as well as its legs and paws are to be covered with relatively shorter hair.

Respectively, the back of the forelegs and hind legs is to display a somewhat longer fur length which extends out to the pastern and hock. Faults are called out when the showing of the coat include silky, soft, woolly, curly, an open coat or an outer coat showing to be too long to meet association standards.

Color

The variations in color of the GSD are plenty and it has been permissible to show dogs which sport most colors of its breed spectrum. Rich, strong and solid colors are given preference. Washed out colors such as blue, silver or pale shades are serious faults which are called out.
A white GS is to be immediately disqualified.

Gait

The structure and physique of a GSD was developed to meet the requirements it needs to carry out tasks it is utilized for and shows of which it displays great ability and dexterity. It is a trotting canine - its gait is flexible, elastic, extended, outreaching and seemingly effortlessly rhythmic and smooth, covering the maximum area of ground with lengthy strides of both forelegs and hind legs.

When at a trot the canine is still able to cover more ground with longer strides. It moves with ease and visible power displaying precise coordination and accurate balance, hence the gait movement is seen to the steady motion of a well-oiled machine.

The feet traverse closely to the ground on both its forward reach and backward push. In order for the canine to meet the requirements of this kind of ideal movement, the development of the GS ligaments as well as proper muscular built should be good and these are imperative for it to obtain balance and agility judges seek.

Its hindquarters carry a powerful forward thrust through the rear which moderately lifts the whole canine's body and propels its carriage forward.

Passing the imprint left behind by the front feet and reaching far under, the hind feet takes hold of the ground;

then the dog's' stifle, hock and upper thigh is introduced to the orchestrated movement and sweeps back, with the stroke of the back legs finishing with the GS foot still close to the ground in a follow-through which shows smooth and elegant.

The overreach of the back legs usually requires one hind foot to pass outside and the other hind foot to pass inside the path or trail of the forefeet. Such a movement is not found to be faulty unless the locomotion is displayed crabwise with the canine's body moving sideways and out of the straight, normal line of movement.

Transmission

The classical smooth, flow of the GSD gait is maintained with utmost firmness and strength of the back. The total effort of the back quarter is carried through to the front quarter through the back, loin and withers. When at full trot, the back of the GS must remain steadfast, firm and leveled sans roll, whip, roach or sway. Topline showing to be unleveled with withers displayed lower than the GS hip is an immediate fault.

The GSD's shoulders must open to the fullest extent to compensate and make up for the forward thrusting motion given off by the canine's hindquarters. The forelegs are to reach out near to the ground in a lengthy stride that is in harmony with that of its hindquarters. The canine does not step on extensively, distant and separate parallel lines; instead it gathers its feet inward toward the midline of its body when in trot so as to maintain its precision balance.

The feet of the GSD, when in movement do not cross over nor do they strike, but should instead track closely. When viewed from the front, the forelegs function at the beginning of the canine shoulder joint to the dog's pad in a straight line. When scrutinized from behind, the back legs of the GSD should function from its hip joint to its pad in a straight line. Faults of gait and movement, whether from rearm side or front will be counted as a fault.

Disqualifications

Hanging or cropped ears are immediately disqualified from showing. GSD canines sporting noses which are not predominantly black are immediate candidates for disqualification. An undershot jaw is also up for immediate disqualification. White GSDs are also immediately disqualified from showing. Any GSD canine displaying hostility and that which attempts to bite the judge is, henceforth, disqualified from showing as well.

Chapter Eight: Breeding Your German Shepherd

Are you prepared in breeding your German Shepherd dog? One must be fully prepared before breeding. Breeding involves many veterinarian bills, it's important for you to have a financial capability. Newborn puppies also need to a lot of attention and caring. Breeding will challenge your physical, emotional and financial aspect. Even the best breeders experience loss. Read on if you really want to become a breeder but take note that there are a lot of things that you should know. This chapter will give you an idea of breeding one.

Basic Dog Breeding Information

The first rule that to you have to understand and follow is that breeding is best left to professional breeders. But of course, it is also essential that you know the basics of breeding a dog. A lot of things are involved, and it is important that you know your responsibilities and all the things that you need to observe to ensure that the breeding will produce healthy German Shepherd puppies.

There is somewhat a high level of loss in puppies. This is caused by different kinds of reasons, and can also happen in any breed not only on German Shepherd dogs, but this happens more often in toy breeds. Anyone who is breeding must understand and accept that puppies may die inexplicably at times. It is heartbreaking and tragic of course.

When Dogs Mate

When a female dog or what they termed it as the 'bitch' is in heat, there are a few signs that can point towards her beginning this process. Below are the following signs you will notice:

- Being nervous
- Easily spooked
- Easily distracted
- Urinating more than usual

Her personality may also alter due to the abrupt change in her hormones. Male dogs are ready to breed from the age of 18 months to 4/5 years old according to breeding dogs Info center. An interesting fact about male dogs is that when they hit the age around 10 years old, the semen they produce will not be capable of impregnating a female.

Tips for Breeding Your German Shepherd Dogs

Now that you know the basics about breeding dogs you can learn the specifics about German Shepherd breed. The German Shepherd dog has a gestation period lasting about 50 - 60 days (2 – 3 months).

The gestation period is the period of time following conception during which the puppies develop in the mother's uterus. The average litter size for the German Shepherd breed is between 8 to 15 puppies.

To increase your chances of a successful breeding, you need to keep track of your German Shepherd dog's estrus cycle. Once your female reaches the point of ovulation, you can introduce her to the male dog and let nature take its course. Breeding behavior varies slightly from one breed to another, but you can expect the male dog to mount the female from behind (as long as she is receptive). If the breeding is successful, conception will occur and the gestation period will begin.

While the puppies are developing inside your female German Shepherd's uterus, you need to take special care to make sure the female is properly nourished. You do not need to make changes to your dog's diet until the fourth or fifth week of pregnancy. At that point you should slightly increase her daily rations in an amount proportionate to her weight gain. It is generally best to offer your dog free feeding because she will know how much she needs to eat. Make sure your dog's diet is high in protein as well as calories and fat to support the development of her puppies – calcium is also very important.

German vs. American Breeding Guidelines

The sort of GS you will get, if acquiring a puppy, will bear slight differences depending on which breeder you choose. You will have to decide whether you'd like to work with a German or American GS breeder.

German breeders purposely breed GSD to enhance and bring out their working abilities whilst maintaining the traditional look of the German Shepherd. A GS has to pass a battery of test in order to prove he is at par with the ideal attributes of a GS up to the mental and physical benchmarks it is known for. The German bred GS have a tendency to have a stronger, driven personality and is more energetic.

On the other hand, American breeders are geared more toward breeding the GS for its appearance with the intention of achieving show dog champions. Rather than breeding the GS for its uncanny abilities and talents, American breeders aim to highlight the distinctive look of the German Shepherd.

GS followers and aficionados remark that American-bred GS are much calmer than their German counterparts but critics contend that these dogs have lost its talents of being a traditional working GS on the job and tend to be more prone to behavioral problems such as separation anxiety.

Chapter Nine: Keeping Your German Shepherd Healthy

The modern day breed German Shepherd is criticized by many for veering away from the original ideology of Max von Stephanitz's German Shepherd. In his mind the dogs should primarily be bred to be working dogs. He believed that breeding these canines has to be stringently controlled to avert defects from the onset. Above all else, he believed that German Shepherds should be bred for its professional working ability as well as its innate intelligence.

Based in the United Kingdom, The Kennel Club, is enmesh with German Shepherd breeding clubs about the show-strain breed and its soundness. The show-strain canines have been bred and developed sporting an extremely sloping back (topline) that causes poor gait of its hind legs. Those used commonly used as service dogs or the Working Pedigree line; usually keep the traditional straight back lines of the breed.

This argument was given rise when the issue was brought up in the BBC documentary Pedigree Dogs Exposed, which mentioned that the critics of this breed describe the canine as: half dog and half frog". They were described to be "not normal" by an orthopedic vet who witnessed a footage of the show ring.

The Kennel Club's stance on the issue was quoted to read "this issue of soundness is not a simple difference of opinion. It is the fundamental issue of the breed's essential conformation and movement". And from hence, coming to an agreement, The Kennel Club had made the decision to retrain judges to penalize dogs who suffer from these problems.

Other common problems this breed displays are hip dysplasia and hemophilia which the Kennel Club strongly insists on more testing to be carried out.

Health Issues of the GSD

Determining health concerns which may plague your GS canine is something you, as eventual caregiver, must know and understand. Being aware of these conditions not only empower you to be selective when choosing breeders to deal with - understanding these ailments and symptoms of such gives you a better advantage of avoiding what needs to be avoided.

Common health ailments that plague GS dogs are the outcome of the improper breeding practices early in the breed's existence, although it was deemed important to preserve the breed's other traits. One of the more common medical conditions of the GS is elbow and hip dysplasia which could lead to the canine enduring pain later in its life and may cause dog arthritis. The University of Zurich conducted a study and discovered that 45% of the working police dogs were affected by a degenerative condition of spinal stenosis; however the sample examined was small.

19.1% of GS were found by the Orthopedic Foundation for Animals to be affected by hip dysplasia. Because of their large and open nature of its ears, GS are not susceptible to ear infections because there is no fur to obstruct the outer ear canal which would hold debris or moisture. A recent UK survey showed the median life span of GS to be 10.95 years which is just about right for a canine of their size.

The neurological disease, Degenerative Myelopathy, happens with regularity specifically in this breed which suggests that the GS breed is a sort predisposed to it. To rule out or detect this neurological disease, an inexpensive saliva test has been made available to screen for degenerative myelopathy. The test looks for the mutated gene responsible for and seen in canines with degenerative myelopathy.

In the United Kingdom, a small study revealed 16% of asymptomatic young GSD to be homozygous to the mutation of the disease with 38% of the lot identified as carriers.

With the advent of the screening test, the disease is better identified and can be bred out successfully from breeds which have a higher likelihood to acquire. It is recommended to give this test to predisposed breeds. The test can also be carried out using DNA samples from any canine using collected saliva samples which can be obtained by swabbing the inside of the canine's cheek with the aid of a sterile cotton swab.

Prospective German Shepherd buyers can ask for the test to be carried out by any breeder now that a test has been made available. Potential GS dog caregivers may also purchase this testing kit from a breeder known to test their canines.

In addition, GS have a higher propensity than usual to acquire Von Willebrand disease. This is a common inherited bleeding disorder. Also detected in this breed is exocrine pancreatic insufficiency (EPI) which is a disease of the pancreas and is degenerative. 1% of the US GSD population is estimated to suffer from this disease. Pancreatic supplements given with food are the usual treatment of this disease.

Bonus Chapter:

The Unwavering Popularity of the German Shepherd

The GS of today owes part of its popularity to a tiny GS pup that was rescued by Corporal Lee Duncan from a bomb and bullet riddled breeding kennel in France during the trying times of WWI. When the war ended, Corporal Duncan brought home the puppy to his Los Angeles home, trained him and transformed the little pup to one of the most loved dogs in show business, Rin Tin Tin.

The Rin Tin Tin character went on to perform in countless movies and received close to 10,000 fan letters each week at the height of its stardom.

Reliable, Trustworthy, Loyal, Focused and Hardworking

Remember that the GS wears many hats apart from being actors and landing acting parts in TV and movies. The reliably trustworthy German Shepherd is dauntless when on the job and will not be distracted by anything that may try to interrupt its attention - ensuring a good measure of pure professionalism at work.

The GSD in all its versatility guides and assists the hearing and visually impaired making sure their ward is safe, sound and secure in placing trust on the canine. It bravely gives chase to, captures and detains criminals on the run and obediently waits for backup assistance from its two-legged, uniformed counterparts. It has served and continues to gallantly give its service during military, police and rescue operations.

The GS is utilized as messenger, bomb sniffing dog, and has provided loving comfort to homesick soldiers stationed overseas. It serves as lookout and watchdog to its guardians. It herds sheep stock and protects the farm animals from would-be thieves and hungry predators.

It assists in curbing the transport of contrabands and sniffs out illegal substances which may pose a threat to security and lives. It pays visits, gives comfort and keeps the ailing in high spirits with its warm companionship. These are the many jobs the GSD has and it has certainly proved itself worthy of the trust we give to it.

During the horrific attack on the Twin Towers, German Shepherds worked side by side with their human counterparts, searching for survivors trapped under rubble. It's presence at the site of the attack was also a great source of comfort for those toiling in the thick of the action and to grieving families alike.

This canine of great repute may embody some of the best qualities and traits of a dog, but the GS is not suited for everyone. Since the GS was bred primarily as a working dog, its high-energy requires a lot of physical activity and exercise. Without its much needed exercise the GS will likely express frustration and boredom in manners you won't like such as chewing on random things and loud barking. Be sure that if you are set on acquiring a GS that you are equally as active and ready to jump up and out of the house at a moment's notice.

The GS is known to sometimes have a suspicious nature and can be quite aloof around strangers. It is a great watchdog and protector but it isn't the kind of family dog who'll go out of its way to welcome guests with open arms.

In order to forego this tedious and often frustrating scenario early exposure to many various situations and human interaction from the onset of puppyhood will help integrate the dog with your kin, your closest friends and other pets. The GS can learn to be more tolerant of new people and take unfamiliar situations in stride if training is introduced in the early formative weeks of the pup.

Popularity

The demand for the GS has risen in recent times and presently continues to garner and gain better favor and much more admirers.

Fifty four German Shepherds were registered in 1919, when the United Kingdom Kennel accepted the breed. This number grew exponentially to 8,000 by 1926. After the decline of WWI, the breed gained a wider audience and following and was given better international recognition. The soldiers who returned from war spoke highly of the breed. The German Shepherd dog-character-actors Rin Tin Tin and Strongheart were instrumental in furthering its popularity.

Queen of Switzerland, as fondly called by its guardians, was the first German Shepherd Dog to be registered in the United States. A decline in the breed's popularity was noted in the late 1920's when the offspring of Queen of Switzerland suffered from defects resulting from poor breeding procedures.

Clamoring for the German Shepherd once again rose after the German Shepherd Sieger Pfeffer von Bern, successively became the Grand Victor in American Kennel Club dog shows in 1937 and 1938. This was a short-lived period of raised popularity and it once again declined at the end of WWII, largely due to anti-German sentiment.
They slowly regained popularity until 1933. This was when the German Shepherd moved up on the popularity list and sat at a comfortable third place in the US.

The German Shepherd, as of 2012, has risen to become the second most popular canine in the US. To add to this, the GS breed is amongst the most popular as well in other registries. The physique of the German Shepherd is made for competitions like agility trials, dog shows and well suited for athletic competition.

The GSD - A Hit in Popular Culture

German Shepherds have been widely employed as actors in an assortment of media. Strongheart became one of the earliest canines to grace the silver screen and was quickly followed by the GS considered to be the most popular of its sort, Rin Tin Tin in 1922.These two dog actors and movie stars each have stars on the Hollywood Walk of Fame. In the timeless Canadian series, The Littlest Hobo, German Shepherds were used as actors.

Ace the Bat-Hound appeared alongside crime fighter Batman in the Batman comic book series from 1955 up through 1964. His appearances were sporadic between the years 1964 to 2007.

Inspector Rex is a German Shepherd who stars in the procedural drama program, Austrian Police, which has been the recipient of countless awards. The show where the GS Rex assists the Vienna Kriminalpolizei homicide unit was aired in various languages throughout the world.

Captain Max Von Stephanitz and The GS History: Glance Back In Time

The German Shepherd is a comparatively new breed dating its beginnings back to 1899 and the canine owes its life and longevity to one man. Captain Max von Stephanitz, a career captain in the German cavalry, immediately recognized the natural intelligence and docile obedience of the canine and set out on a goal of developing a herding dog that would be unmatched by other breeds.

Farmers in Germany and the rest of Europe centuries prior to von Stephanitz, relied heavily on herding dogs to help steer and protect their herds. Some of the dogs employed for the job displayed exemplary abilities and skill. Sheepherders on a quest to breed their bitches to a noteworthy sire would travel for days to carry out this task. However, there was no interest in developing the herding canines of the region to bring about a unique and distinct breed of working dogs.

When von Stephanitz retired from military service in 1898, he commenced to carve out his second career and what would be his greatest passion - experimenting with canine breeding methods to develop a superior German herding canine. He travelled throughout Germany to attend canine shows and observe herding dogs of the German nature. He also studied the breeding techniques of the British who were noted for their superb herding canines.

Having travelled far and wide, Von Stephanitz came across many fine herding dogs that were capable, athletic or intelligent. But he was disappointed that he had yet to come across a canine that would display and bear all the traits he supposed would be classified as the ultimate working canine.

Hektor a.k.a. Horand - The Populator

On a particular day in 1899, whilst visiting a dog show, von Stephanitz chanced upon and spotted a wolfish-looking canine that caught his fancy. He promptly made an offer for the canine and brought it home. This was Hektor who was later renamed Horand von Grafeth. The canine's visibly powerful physique and intelligence left a deep impression on the captain turned breeder/aficionado that he went on to found the Verein fur deutsche Schaferhunde society and establish a breed from Horand's descendents.

Originally intended to be developed as herd dogs, the canine's popularity faded slightly as Germany became more and more industrialized. Von Stephanitz was set on making this breed be the best working dog breed. This is when he surmised that the dog's future lay in police and military service.

Utilizing his military connections to the dog's advantage, the former captain managed to convince the German government to employ the breed. And so, the GS went on to serve in the armed forces of Germany during WWI as a Red Cross dog, rescuer, guard, sentry, carrier of supplies and messenger.

Final Thoughts

Now that you have completely poured over each page of this book, the author trusts that the information herein has helped you come closer to making the crucial decision of buying or taking in a German Shepherd dog. It is the hope of this writer that you, dear reader, have gained better understanding of the German Shepherd Dog breed and is now quite aware of what to expect when expecting a GSD.

The trustworthy, obedient German Shepherd canine will surely reveal itself to be a sound addition to the family, who with it brings the loyal companionship of a true friend. The keen and accurate senses of the canine will give you and your loved ones an extra veil of protection. Its natural protective instincts - if trained well - will give you a true sense of security in the presence of danger.

Whether you opt to show and display your GSD or not, keep in mind that the GSD is your friend and companion, foremost. Make these forays to shows fun and stress-free and do not let these shows be the center of your lifelong buddy's existence.

You will go through challenges as any household does when welcoming an addition to the family dynamics, but you will never forget the days when the universe remembers to reward and silently thank you for caring for one of its own special creations. Sharing your family, home, resources, love and company are the intangibly vital ingredients to living a good life and your new German Shepherd. While unfamiliar with most the human language, will not be at a loss to methods, manners and ways, to how it would express its undying gratitude toward the loving kindness and care you shower it.

Index

M

N

O

P

S

T

Photo Credits

Page 1 Photo by adamkontor via Pixabay.com, https://pixabay.com/en/dog-animal-pets-german-shepherd-eb-2144031/

Page 9 Photo by christels via Pixabay.com, https://pixabay.com/en/dog-german-shepherd-close-up-2035393/

Page 24 Photo by greekfood - tamystika via Pixabay.com, https://pixabay.com/en/german-shepherd-dog-dog-lying-down-1970026/

Page 35 Photo by skeeze via Pixabay.com, https://pixabay.com/en/dog-german-shepherd-snow-flakes-903990/

Page 44 Photo by toinny via Pixabay.com, https://pixabay.com/en/german-shepherd-dogs-play-beach-1805629/

Page 53 Photo by christels via Pixabay.com, https://pixabay.com/en/dog-german-shepherd-animal-branch-1871985/

Page 68 Photo by Pexels via Pixabay.com, https://pixabay.com/en/german-shepherd-mix-rescue-dog-1845744/

Page 82 Photo by Thomas43 via Pixabay.com,

https://pixabay.com/en/lake-berger-pet-nature-water-1273840/

Page 88 Photo by cortez13 via Pixabay.com, https://pixabay.com/en/dog-german-shepherd-autumn-foliage-1134629/

Page 94 Photo by 117271 via Pixabay.com, https://pixabay.com/en/german-shepherd-dog-pet-happy-232393/

References

German Shepherd Dog – Dogtime.com
<http://dogtime.com/dog-breeds/german-shepherd-dog#/slide/1 >

Choosing A Dog: German Shepherd – Petbreeds.com
<http://dogs.petbreeds.com/l/70/German-Shepherd >

German Shepherd - Wikipedia
<https://en.wikipedia.org/wiki/German_Shepherd >

German Shepherd Dog – Dogbreedinfo.com
<http://www.dogbreedinfo.com/germanshepherd.htm >

German Shepherd Dog – AKC.org
<http://www.akc.org/dog-breeds/german-shepherd-dog/>

German Shepherd – Petmd.com
<http://www.petmd.com/dog/breeds/c_dg_german_shepherd>

German Shepherd Food and Nutrition
<http://www.german-shepherd-us.com/german-shepherd-food.html>

**The History and Origin of the German Shepherd Dog –
German Shepherd Rescue Elite**
<http://gsrelite.co.uk/the-history-origin-of-the-german-
shepherd-dog/>

**History and Origin of the German Shepherd Dog –
German Shepherd Rescue UK**
<https://www.germanshepherdrescue.co.uk/german-
shepherd-history-i-150.html>

German Shepherd Dog History – German Shepherds ETC
<http://germanshepherdsetc.com/german-shepherd-dog-
history/>

German Shepherd Dog Breed – Pawculture.com
<http://www.pawculture.com/breed-basics/dog-
breeds/german-shepherd-dog-breed/>

German Shepherd Dog – Breed History
<http://www.nsgsdc.com/breedhistory.shtml>

**Mating a German Shepherd Dog –
GermanShepherdDogsToday.com**
<http://www.germanshepherddogstoday.com/matingagerm
anshepherddog.html>

The German Shepherd – Canismajor.com

<http://www.canismajor.com/dog/germansh.html>

GSD Standards - Germanshepherdguide.com

<http://www.germanshepherdguide.com/the-gsd-standards.html>

Work, Sports and Activities - Germanshepherdguide.com

<http://www.germanshepherdguide.com/work-sports-and-activities.html>

Feeding Baby
Cynthia Cherry
978-1941070000

Axolotl
Lolly Brown
978-0989658430

Dysautonomia, POTS
Syndrome
Frederick Earlstein
978-0989658485

Degenerative Disc
Disease Explained
Frederick Earlstein
978-0989658485

Sinusitis, Hay Fever,
Allergic Rhinitis Explained
Frederick Earlstein
978-1941070024

Wicca
Riley Star
978-1941070130

Zombie Apocalypse
Rex Cutty
978-1941070154

Capybara
Lolly Brown
978-1941070062

Eels As Pets
A Complete Guide
Where to buy, species, aquarium, supplies, diet, care, tank setup, and more!

Lolly Brown

Eels As Pets
Lolly Brown
978-1941070167

Scabies and Lice Explained
Causes, Prevention, Treatment, and Remedies All Covered!

Information including symptoms, care, removal, eggs, home remedies, in pets, natural treatment, life cycle, infestation, cure specific, and much more.

Frederick Earlstein

Scabies and Lice Explained
Frederick Earlstein
978-1941070017

Saltwater Fish as Pets
A Complete Pet Owner's Guide

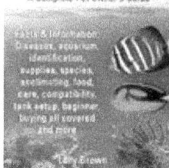

Facts & information, Diseases, aquarium, identification, supplies, species, acclimating, food, care, compatibility, tank setup, beginner buying all covered and more.

Lolly Brown

Saltwater Fish As Pets
Lolly Brown
978-0989658461

Torticollis Explained
A Complete Care Guide

Causes, Symptoms, and Treatment all covered!

Frederick Earlstein

Torticollis Explained
Frederick Earlstein
978-1941070055

Kennel Cough
Lolly Brown
978-0989658409

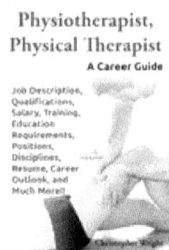

Physiotherapist, Physical
Therapist
Christopher Wright
978-0989658492

Rats, Mice, and Dormice
As Pets
Lolly Brown
978-1941070079

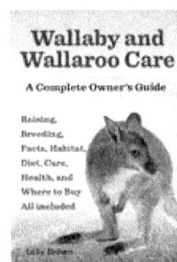

Wallaby and Wallaroo Care
Lolly Brown
978-1941070031

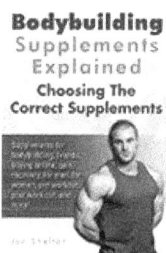

Bodybuilding Supplements
Explained
Jon Shelton
978-1941070239

Demonology
Riley Star
978-19401070314

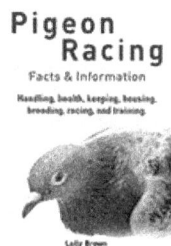

Pigeon Racing
Lolly Brown
978-1941070307

Dwarf Hamster
Lolly Brown
978-1941070390

Cryptozoology
Rex Cutty
978-1941070406

Eye Strain
Frederick Earlstein
978-1941070369

Inez The Miniature Elephant
Asher Ray
978-1941070353

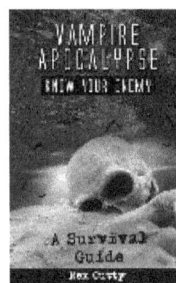

Vampire Apocalypse
Rex Cutty
978-1941070321